THE TRUE STORY OF THE LEADEN STATUARY;

OR,

A CURIOUS CHAPTER IN ECONOMIC HISTORY.

BY

DAVID A. WELLS.

Reprinted from *The New York World* of May 11th, 1874.

NEW YORK:

1874.

THE

TRUE STORY

OF THE

LEADEN STATUARY;

OR,

A CURIOUS CHAPTER IN ECONOMIC HISTORY.

BY

DAVID A. WELLS.

Reprinted from *The New York World* of May 11th, 1874.

NEW YORK:

1874.

"A story as amusing as a novel is scarcely what we are accustomed to expect from the sedate pen of our excellent economist, Mr. DAVID A. WELLS. But that is precisely what we are indebted to him for this morning, as the brightest of our fairest readers will admit, who hate figures, skip statistics and would disclaim the ballot if it involved learning economics. Mr. WELLS has dug up and relates for us the True Story of the Leaden Statuary. Its moral draws itself, as in the case of all good and well told stories."—*New York World*, May 11th, 1874.

A CURIOUS CHAPTER IN ECONOMIC HISTORY.

THERE is an amusing old story told of the magistrates of a certain country town in France, who, before the days of street lamps and gas, and as a better security against the unlawful acts of "vagrom men," passed an ordinance that "no citizen should walk out after dark without a lantern," and that disobedience of the law should entail a heavy penalty. The watch, vigilant in the performance of duty, accordingly arrested, the first night after the law took effect, a well known and estimable individual, but of waggish propensities, and hauled him up before the local Dogberry on charge of having broken the statute. The defendant, however, on being asked why punishment should not be inflicted upon him, averred that he had committed no offence, and, in support of his plea, produced a lantern. It being rejoined that the lantern had no candle, he next maintained that the law did not require that the lantern should contain any candle; and the statute being examined and the defence found valid, the arrested party was dismissed and the law so amended as to read, "that no citizen should hereafter walk out after dark, without a lantern and a candle." The next night the same person being found walking in darkness was again arrested and arraigned, but again maintained that he had committed no offence; and, in proof thereof, produced a lantern and showed that it contained a candle. "But the candle," said Dogberry, "is not lighted." "And the law," rejoined the wag, "does not require that it should be;" and this interpretation being found correct, the accused was once more discharged and the statute further amended so as to read, "that no citizen should hereafter walk out after dark without a lantern and a candle in it, and that the candle should be lighted."

The next night the same incorrigible and troublesome person was again brought up before the Court, and this time both watch and magistrate thought they had a sure thing of it; for, to all appearances, he had not on this occasion even made a pretence of complying with the law. But the triumph of the officials was of brief duration, for, to their utter disgust and amazement, the accused drew from his capacious coat pocket a dark lantern, and showed that it not only contained a candle, but that the candle was lighted and burning. Warned by this threefold experience, the statute was for a third time amended, and this time so fully and clearly that no further practical jokes were attempted, and the majesty of the law remained unassailed.

As thus told the above story is manifestly a broad burlesque, even in its application to stupid French "country officials," and without further foundation than the imagination of its author. But it is nevertheless a most curious and amusing circumstance that it has been reserved to the United States to furnish out of the history of its fiscal legislation a record of actual experience which, in many respects, is the exact and truthful counterpart of the French burlesque; and, as the incidents involved have more than once (but always incorrectly) been alluded to on the floor of Congress, and may be found pertinent to prospective legislation and debate in respect to custom house reforms and irregularities, it is proposed to now embody them for the first time, and, as a contribution to economic literature, in the form of a correct and complete narration.

Between the years 1816 and 1828, encouraged by the imposition of a low duty on imported metallic lead, the manufacture of white lead as a basis for paints came into existence in the United States and developed with great rapidity, the principal seats of the business being the cities of New York, Philadelphia and Baltimore. But about the years 1826–28 the discovery of the lead mines at Galena, Ill., became generally known, and as the first reports were to the effect that the deposits were of such unparalleled richness, purity, magnitude and easy accessibility as to make it only a question of time when the whole world, from sheer inability to compete, became wholly dependent for its supplies of lead on this one locality, it was at once considered desirable by many people to establish, so far as fiscal legislation could do it, a most extraordinary economic principle, and one which from that day to this has proved popular in all our tariff enactments; and this was to make the discovery or recognition of the existence of any great natural advantages—either in the way of mines, soils, climatic advantages, forests, means of intercommunication or national characteristics—the immediate occasion for cursing the country by the creation and imposition of some new tax, thereby making dear what was before cheap, and endeavoring to work up to a state of abundance through conditions of scarcity artificially created and unnecessarily perpetuated. In this particular instance the principle was exemplified by raising the duty on lead imported in pigs and bars from one cent a pound to three cents; and to this extent increasing to the consumer the price of the raw material, whether of foreign or domestic origin, and of all manufactured products in which lead entered as the principal constituent. As the duty was not at the same time correspondingly advanced on the import of white lead, and as the lead mining interests of Galena were not prepared to supply at any price the immediate demand thus artificially created for their products in the domestic market, the American manufacturers of white lead all at once found their business threatened with utter destruction; and, with intellects preternaturally sharpened by a prospective loss of a large invested capital, they looked shrewdly about to see in what manner they could save and protect themselves.

And putting on their spectacles, and scrutinizing carefully the entire tariff, as modified by the special Act of 1828 referred to, they soon discovered that the Government, while effectually closing and barring up the big door by which foreign lead could be imported, had inadvertently left wide open a smaller door beside it, inasmuch as while Congress had prescribed a duty of three cents per pound on lead imported in pigs and bars, they left a prior duty of fifteen per cent. *ad valorem* on the import of *old lead* fit only to be remanufactured, unrepealed and in force. Those were the days of packet ships and slow communication with the Old World; but we may readily believe that no time was unnecessarily wasted by those interested in this discovery; and at the earliest practicable moment afterwards agents of nearly every important American house engaged in the importation of metals—Barclay & Livingston, Boorman, Johnson & Co., Hoffman, Bend & Co., Phelps & Peck, William Wright & Co., and many lesser firms—were ransacking the markets of Europe for the purchase and shipment to the United States of old lead. Of course, the legitimate market supplies, never great, of this peculiar article soon gave out, but the agents and correspondents of the American houses being Yankees, proved fully equal to the emergency, and a scheme was forthwith devised to replenish the stock by exchanging new lead for old, and contracts in more than one instance, for example, were actually entered into and carried out for stripping from extensive factories in different parts of England their old lead roofing—lead being then used more extensively than now in the place of slate—and replacing it without expense to the owners with new roofing on condition of receiving the old material.

In the course of time the old lead thus collected began to make its appearance on this side of the Atlantic, and arriving in large quantities—almost by the ship load—at the ports of New York and Boston, naturally attracted the attention of the custom house authorities, who at first demurred to its entry at the low duty of 15 per cent. *ad valorem*. The matter, however, being referred to the Treasury Department at Washington, an answer soon came back that the position of the merchants was unimpeachable, but the Department would have the law amended as soon as possible.

But the merchants by this time, in studying up the fiscal legislation of Congress in respect to lead in pigs and old lead, had made another discovery—and that was that the tariff Act in force was mandatory to this further effect, namely, that if any person or persons should import musket balls or leaden bullets into the United States they should pay to the custom authorities a duty on the same of 15 per cent. *ad valorem*, and, in default thereof, the goods should be forfeited and the importers be punished. Like good citizens, therefore, the merchants made haste to obey the law, and their agents in Europe being duly instructed, lost no time in buying up all the musket balls and leaden bullets they could find for sale, and when the foreign markets were exhausted they had musket balls of the regulation weight and calibre largely manufactured, and all were duly shipped as fast as possible to the United States. Again the custom house authorities objected, but again came back the response from Washington that the law was explicit in respect to the 15 per cent. duty, and that nothing could be done in the way of restraining the importation of leaden bullets in place of pig lead until Congress had provided further legislation on the subject.

But the tariff Acts in force from 1828 to 1832 were, however, almost as much a mystery and a muddle of perplexity as are the Acts under which the customs are at present administered, and it was only after continuous study and investigation that their full depth of meaning and of wisdom could become evident. But the success attending the import of old lead and musket balls had been so remarkable, and the preservation and resuscitation of the "white lead" business so encouraging, that the merchants were stimulated to further fiscal investigations; and again putting on their spectacles, they discovered two other remarkable provisions of the then existing tariff which heretofore had not been considered of much importance. These provisions related, the one to "leaden weights" of all descriptions, and the other to "sounding leads," and were to the effect that if any person imported any of these articles into the United States he should pay on the same a duty of 15 per cent. *ad valorem.*

It seems almost unnecessary to relate in detail the consequence of these discoveries, but it sufficeth to say that those were the good old days when false standards were far more of an abomination than they now are, and it was astonishing how great a demand all at once appeared to have been created in the United States for full, fresh, and new sets of leaden weights (from half an ounce to fifty-six pounds and upwards, but notably of the heavier denominations), which had not had their accuracy impaired by continuous use and abrasion. If the exact truth, moreover, could now be known, it might also appear that many persons at that time (especially in the cities of New York and Boston) had somehow become indoctrinated with the idea that the possession of more "weights" would in some way increase the quantity of things to be weighed—in the same way as the progressive men of the present day have brought themselves to believe that the possession of more paper money will increase the value and quantity of the things that this same money can buy. Those were the days, also, when clocks were high and stood in corners rather than upon mantels, and were moved by weights rather than by springs, and our ancestors of forty years ago—and none knew better than they that "time is money"—all at once seemed possessed with the desire to have more clocks, for the import of heavy leaden clock weights, with iron hooks neatly fitted to one end, and which *prima facie* could be only used for the manufacture of clocks, all at once increased and rapidly became a business of magnitude.

Navigators also about this time, it might be inferred, became more intelligent; or, if not more intelligent, then, through a desire to save their insurance premiums, more cautious; or, if not these, then the desire of American geographical students to study more accurately the sea bottom, might have been abnormally stimulated; for in what other way could an excessive and unusual import of deep sea sounding leads be accounted for?—leads small, leads large, leads of two ounces weight, leads of seventy pounds weight, leads a few inches in length up to leads two feet in length—all with an eyelet at one end for the sounding line attachment and a cavity at the other for the reception of the tallow, by the agency of which specimens were to be brought up from the sea bottom.

But the custom house authorities were practical men. They indulged in no philosophical reflections as to any abstract possible uses of the imported articles in question. They saw in all of them lead and lead only—and on lead, in the interests of the Galena mines and of the revenue, they wanted a duty of three cents per pound. They accordingly, as opportunity offered, seized and refused to deliver the exceptionally large invoices of "clock weights" "scale weights" and "sounding leads," and the appeal, as usual, from their proceedings went up from the merchants to Washington. But if the custom house officials were practical men, the Treasury magnates at the capital, on the other hand, were strict constructionists, and as they found the statute written so they interpreted it; and in all cases the arrested importations of the merchants were, after a little delay, restored and admitted to entry; and in at least one case, where three cents per pound had been paid under protest on the above mentioned leaden articles, the difference between that sum and fifteen per cent. was returned to the merchant by the Treasury. In fact, as "sea stores" of all descriptions were then on the free list, "sounding leads" might have been claimed to be exempt from all imposts; but the merchants were generous, and this question does not appear to have been raised.

It is not to be denied, nevertheless, that by this time lead had got to be a very irritating topic to a Federal official; and indeed it was only necessary to say "lead" to a United States district attorney, a collector or revenue inspector, to seriously disturb his mental equanimity. An opportunity to retaliate upon their mercantile tormentors was therefore earnestly sought for, and before long such an opportunity seemed to present itself. A prominent New York house in the metal trade, which, in connection with some half dozen or more leading firms, had been engaged in importing old lead, musket bullets, sounding leads, clock weights, and the like, and passing them, under a strict but legal construction of the statute, at fifteen per cent. *ad valorem*, imported on one occasion, during the period under consideration but subsequent to the events narrated, an invoice of stereotype metal. Now, stereotype metal was then on the free list of the tariff, and subject to no duty, and in this particular instance the importation had been made in consequence of a direct order received from one of the largest type founders in New York; but as it came in pigs or bars, was in unusual quantity, and consisted merely of lead mixed with comparatively small proportions of antimony and bismuth, the custom house officials conceived the idea that it was only a new device of the enemy to take advantage of the faulty statute, and that the ultimate intent was to remelt the stereotype metal, separate its several constituents, and then dispose of the lead independently. The whole invoice was accordingly seized, and suit commenced in the United States District Court for its forfeiture, the Government having previously ascertained, by means of an analysis of a sample bar, made at their request by the then famous New York chemist, old Dr. Chilton, that the metal contained somewhat more than eighty per cent. of lead. The District Attorney at that time was Price, afterwards best known for some financial irregularities. The merchants, of course, resisted, and on the day of trial appeared in court with the type founder on whose account the metal was ordered, and other experts, to prove that the import and prospective use of the metal were entirely legitimate. The Government opened their case by stating their assumption that the metal was not imported for the manufacture of stereotypes but for the purpose of defrauding the revenue, and, calling as their first witness Dr. Chilton, examined him somewhat as follows:

District Attorney—What is your profession? Dr. Chilton—A chemist.

Q. Where were you educated? A. In Edinburgh, and have followed for many years my profession in New York.

Q. Have you made an analysis of this imported metal [at the same time referring to one of the bars included in the invoice]? A. I have.

Q. Of what does it consist? A. Of some 80 per cent. of lead; the remainder, antimony, bismuth and tin.

Q. Is it possible to separate these several constituents, as thus mixed, so as to use and sell them separately? A. Perfectly so.

Q. Please tell the Court what, in your opinion, would be about the expense of the operation. A. Rather more than all the materials are worth.

There was silence for a few moments. The District Attorney did not seem to be possessed of a further inquiring spirit. It was a warm summer's day, and the Judge (Betts), after mopping his face with his handkerchief, stretched his head forward, and, somewhat brusquely, asked if Mr. Price had any rebutting testimony, and, on receiving a negative reply, fell back in his chair with the remark, "Then the case had better be dismissed." And dismissed it was.

But the troubles of the custom house officials were not yet ended; and here comes in that portion of this curious series of events which is best known to the public, is the most comical, and which, as has already been remarked, is often referred to in Congressional debates, when topics of the tariff, smugging, or under valuations are under consideration.

The wicked merchants, encouraged by their complete success as law interpreters, had continued their tariff investigations, and had further found among its provisions in force one to the effect that "metal statuary and busts" might be imported free of duty. It was thereupon immediately determined by the merchants that if the American people desired to cultivate their taste, or keep alive the memory of the good and great of former days by adorning their houses and grounds with metal statuary, they ought to have the opportunity of so doing; and, accordingly, large orders were sent to Europe—at that time the exclusive seat of high art—for the manufacture of busts—mainly colossal—of Washington, Lafayette, Napoleon, Moses and the prophets, and not forgetting, also, duplicates or reproductions of the great works of antiquity; and as lead, of all the metals, seemed to possess in the highest degree the qualities of durability, tenacity, cheapness, and facility of being moulded, the statuary in question was directed to be made of lead. It should also be remarked in this connection that lead statuary fifty years ago was not the abnormal exceptional thing it now is. In fact it was then the common material for cheap imagery throughout Europe, when something less expensive than bronze or marble was desired, and filled the place which is now supplied by cast iron and zinc, but which materials fifty years ago were not thought susceptible of ornamental adaptation. And that the lead statuary in question was really ornamental is proved by the circumstance that some of it thus imported is yet in use for ornamental purposes, one piece embellishing at the present time the garden of an eminent banker on Fifth avenue. From such an æsthetic point of view, also, did the prosaic custom house officers regard the first importations of these leaden images, and so might they long have continued to regard them, had the persons in Europe intrusted with their shipment been more careful in respect to packing. But when Washington came up out of the hold of the vessel after a rough voyage with his nose punched in, and Napoleon with his eyes sufficiently askew to require an operation for strabismus, and Moses looking very much like a subject on whom the law ought to be administered rather than an author and administrator of the law, suspicion was naturally excited, and forthwith the statuary was seized and held for forfeiture by the customs authorities. In answer, the importers, as before, pointed to the clear and explicit provision of the tariff then in force—"Metal statuary and busts free"—and urged the Government, if they doubted, to institute a suit. But Mr. Price, the district attorney, had once burned his fingers with cold lead, and persistently refused to bring the matter into court. Thereupon one of New York's then best known merchants and publicists, who still flourishes in a serene old age, caused an invoice of the questionable statuary to be imported into Boston, and arranged with the district attorney of that port to try the issue in respect to its dutiable character. When the trial came on Daniel Webster appeared as counsel for the defence. His speech in answer to Government was very brief but to the point, claiming the law provided for the admission of metal statuary, busts, etc., free, with no limit as to the kind or quantity, and that the imports in question were metal statuary, though made of lead. When the case closed Mr. Webster requested the Judge to charge the jury that they were to decide whether the articles were metal statuary, and if they found that they were, they must bring in a verdict for the defendants. The Judge substantially did as requested, and the jury, in a few minutes after retiring, returned with a verdict for Mr. Leavitt.

The decision in this case practically put an end to the whole controversy. The lead statuary under seizure was released, the import was allowed to go on unrestricted, and, as soon as circumstances permitted, Congress amended the tariff by equalizing the duties on all forms of lead, and at the same time satisfied the white lead manufacturing interest by fully protecting their products from foreign competition.

As this curious story has been heretofore told, the importation of the leaden statuary has been popularly attributed to the agency of the well known New York firm of Phelps, Dodge & Co. This is, however, an error. The firm of Phelps, Dodge & Co. was not at the time of the occurrence of these events in existence; and the old firm that preceded them—namely, that of Phelps & Peck—although large importers of metals, were not concerned in this matter of the leaden images.

It would be a mistake, furthermore, to infer that like muddles and perplexities cease to characterize the tariff when Congress, taught by experience, successively remedied the omissions and commissions of the Act of 1828. On the contrary, there has been hardly a tariff enacted since that time which has not the absurdities of the old lead, the musket balls, the clock weights, the deep-sea leads, and the leaden images in some form repeated. Thus, for example, in the tariff of 1846 a duty was imposed on flaxseed of twenty per cent., but in the tariff of 1857 linseed was made free while flaxseed was charged fifteen per cent. duty. As might have been expected, the import of linseed was always large, but that of flaxseed very small.

Again, in 1864, the manufacturers of spool thread, anxious to shield themselves against all foreign competition, obtained a prohibitory duty on the import of unwound cotton thread or yarn. When the law went into effect it was found that the result of the new duty would be the destruction of the manufacture of fine elastic fabrics, suspenders, gaiters, etc., as well as of certain worsted fabrics, which were dependent on Europe for certain qualities of warp yarns not then manufactured on this side of the Atlantic. The difficulty was, however, got over by an absurd Treasury ruling, that cotton warp or yarn intended for use in the manufacture of elastic worsted or woollen fabrics was not unwound thread or yarn, but a manufacture of cotton "not otherwise provided for."

And, coming down still later, Congress, in 1872, enacted a general reduction of ten per cent. in tariff rates on metals and manufacture of metals—watches and jewelry excepted. It clear, however, that "watch cases" are not "watches," and neither are springs, escapements, wheels, etc., etc., considered separately. The course of trade, therefore, in respect to imported watches, soon adjusted itself as follows: The movements taken out of the cases, packed in separate cartons, but carefully numbered, are, when thus imported, clearly manufactures of metals, and as such entitled to the rebate of ten per cent. In like manner the cases, without the essentials of a watch in them, are nothing but manufactures of metal (gold and silver), and must be also thus treated in respect of duty. Watches, of course, when they come in as watches, pay full duty!!!

Thus the old, old story of the effect of impolitic and absurd restrictions on trade and commerce, the lesson of which Europe through centuries of experience learned and profited by, continues to repeat itself in the fiscal policy of the United States. Let us hope that the result here, too, at no distant day will be what it has been elsewhere, namely, to force men to the conclusion that the best system of taxation is to tax but a few things, and then leave those taxes to diffuse, and adjust, and apportion themselves by the inflexible laws of trade and political economy—and, furthermore, to recognize that no system of government has any just claim to the title of free which arbitrarily takes from its citizens any portion of their property except to defray the State's necessary expenditures.

www.ingramcontent.com/pod-product-compliance
Lightning Source LLC
LaVergne TN
LVHW010834120826
845149LV00016B/1376
* 9 7 8 1 4 1 8 1 9 0 7 5 0 *